Mother Teresa

of Calcutta

Translation by Janet Chevrier

Under the direction of Romain Lizé, Vice President, MAGNIFICAT
Editor, MAGNIFICAT: Isabelle Galmiche
Editor, Ignatius: Vivian Dudro
Assistant to the Editor: Pascale van de Walle
Layout Designer: Le Semeur d'Images - Gilles Malgonne
Production: Thierry Dubus, Sabine Marioni

Original French edition: Mère Térésa de Calcutta
© 2016 by Pierre Téqui éditeur, Paris

Printed in June 2016 by Tien Wah Press, Malaysia
Job number MGN 16020
Printed in compliance with the Consumer Protection Safety Act, 2008.

Francine Bay

Mother Teresa
of Calcutta

Illustrations by
Emmanuel Beaudesson

MAGNIFICAT • Ignatius

A Childhood in Albania

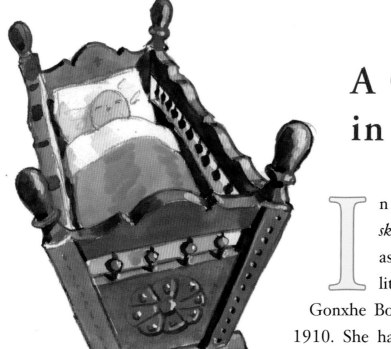

In the town of Skopje (pronounced *sko-piay*), in a country today known as Macedonia, north of Greece, little Anjezë (in English, Agnes) Gonxhe Bojaxhiu was born on August 26, 1910. She had a sister, Age, and a brother, Lazarus, who were a little older than she was. This deeply Christian family lived in Albania, a neighboring country where their father ran several construction companies. Their mother watched carefully over her children's education.

Agnes made her First Communion at the age of five. That day, she felt great love in her heart for all souls. She was a happy little girl, but when she was only eight years old, her father suddenly died. What a tragedy! The family struggled to make ends meet. Agnes' mother went on courageously raising her children, teaching them to help those poorer than themselves. Agnes often went with her mother on visits to the sick or orphans. And beggars were frequently invited to join them for their evening meal.

The village parish, run by the Jesuits, was dedicated to the Sacred Heart of Jesus. The whole family was very active in it. Agnes sang in the choir, played the mandolin, and even took part in plays.

Sometimes, missionaries came to preach. Agnes was so moved by their stories that by the time she was twelve, she was already thinking of following their example. As the years went by, Agnes' desire to consecrate herself to God grew. But how could she be sure of her vocation? Would there be a sign to know that it really came from God?

A priest friend told her, "You will know through joy." With that, Agnes was sure the Lord wanted her to be a missionary, she was so full of joy! Her mother was worried at first, but she finally rejoiced in this vocation and gave her approval.

And so, on September 28, 1928, when Agnes was eighteen, she left Albania, a predominantly Muslim country, to join the missionary Order of the Sisters of Loreto in Ireland. Two months later, the order sent her to India: she was off on a great adventure!

5

In Calcutta

On arriving in Calcutta, a big crowded city, Agnes was overwhelmed by all the poverty. But she did not stay. She boarded a train for the lush green mountains of Darjeeling, where there was a convent of the Sisters of Loreto. They were teaching sisters and had numerous schools throughout the world.

Agnes was admitted as a novice. She gave herself completely to Jesus, and for her, this was happiness!

Two years later, in 1931, Agnes took temporary vows and received the name Sister Mary Teresa, in honor of Saint Thérèse of Lisieux, who had recently been canonized.

Her superiors then sent her as a geography teacher to their high school, Saint Mary's, in Calcutta. It was attended by young women from well-to-do families. Through her enthusiasm, joy, and also firmness, her students came very soon to love her.

They all began calling her "Ma," which means "Mother." On May 24, 1937, "Mother Teresa" professed her perpetual vows, which made her, from then on, "the bride of Jesus for all eternity." How happy she was to repeat those words to herself!

She was also admired for her bright ideas and sense of organization. And so, in 1944, she was the natural choice to become the principal of the high school.

She was pleased to write and tell her mother, who wrote right back, "My dear child, do not forget that if you have left for such a faraway land, it is for the poor."

"Come, Be My Light"

On September 10, 1946, Mother Teresa set off for the train station to go to Darjeeling for her annual retreat.

On her way, she was once again confronted by the extreme poverty of the people. Was that the reason this day was to mark a profound turning point in her life? As a young girl, she had responded with joy to the call of Jesus to be a missionary; on the train she heard "a call within a call." During the trip, she couldn't sleep. Suddenly, she heard a voice. "I was sure it was God's voice," she later wrote, and she added: "The message was clear. I must leave the convent to help the poor by living with them. This was a command, something to be done. Something definite. I knew where I had to be. But I did not know how to get there." Jesus helped Mother Teresa to understand how much he was "thirsty for souls," how much he suffered on seeing everyone's neglect of the poor, when he so greatly desired that they know his special love for them, and love him in return. Jesus begged her, "Come, be my light; I cannot go alone."

When Mother Teresa returned to Calcutta, she went back to work at the high school. But Jesus, speaking to her heart through visions and an inner voice, insistently reminded her of his request.

Mother Teresa decided to confide all this to her superior, who made her wait in order to test her obedience. Fortunately, Mother Teresa had a friend in Father van Exem, a Belgian Jesuit, who spoke to the bishop of Calcutta about her.

At last, on August 8, 1948, Mother Teresa received permission, for a period of one year, to live outside her convent.

Her sisters and her students who loved her so much were very sorry to see her go. On August 17, 1948, Mother Teresa took off the habit of the Sisters of Loreto and put on a sari, the traditional dress of Indian women. Hers was very simple. She found it in the market: a large swathe of white cotton, with just a border of three blue stripes, and on her shoulder she attached a little black crucifix.

Mother Teresa could finally go, as Jesus had asked her to, into the streets to show his love for the poor.

10

The Slums

In her first days in the slums, she visited families, cleaned a few children's sores, and comforted those who were dying the best she could. She stayed for a while with the Little Sisters of the Poor and received basic nurse's training. Every morning, she would go to Mass and then, rosary in hand, set out on her mission to find "the unwanted, the unloved, the uncared for" in whom she sought to see Jesus himself.

One day in the slum of Motijil, Mother Teresa found a child lying in the mud making heartbreaking cries. She scooped it up in her arms and was trying to console it when a woman appeared and immediately accused Mother Teresa of trying to steal her child. Soon, a little crowd gathered: "What's this European woman doing here?" "She's a nun; she's going to take our children away to make them Christians!" A circle of terribly threatening men tightened around Mother Teresa. Were they about to kill her?

At that moment a young man arrived. He told the men that Mother Teresa had nursed him so well two months earlier that he owed his life to her!

The other men backed off; the worst had been avoided in the nick of time, and the young man even offered his services to help Mother Teresa. But this first contact with hostility had been an ordeal!

Yet Mother Teresa returned each day and was so helpful that, in the end, the people living in the slum accepted her.

To Feel Loved

One day, she gathered some children around her, and using very basic means, drawing letters on the ground, she began to teach them to read. They were enthusiastic, and in a few days, there were more than fifty of them! Another day, she arrived with a box full of little soaps: she distributed them to all her new students and showed them how to wash with soap. There were fits of laughter, and their mothers were, after all, delighted to see their children nice and clean!

Mother Teresa was now living very close to the poor, with a Portuguese family who let her have a room in their house.

Above all, she wished to make the poor understand how much God loved them, even if everyone else rejected them. She said, "We think sometimes that poverty is only being hungry, naked and homeless. The poverty of being unwanted, unloved and uncared for is the greatest poverty."

The Missionaries of Charity

One morning, an enormous dump truck arrived in the slum. Escorted by a police car, the truck was headed for the big pile of garbage on which dozens of men and children would scramble every day in search of something to eat or reuse. Armed with loudspeakers, the police ordered them to come down immediately. Mother Teresa rushed to their defense, and the police grudgingly turned away. She managed to turn the situation around completely. This time, the men of the slum applauded her, and even one of those who had still been doubtful of her humbly said, "I was wrong about you, Sister!"

Mother Teresa's love and dedication began winning admiration on all sides. And, one day in 1949—what joy!—a former cook from the high school came to join her in her work, and soon one of her former students too. They were rapidly followed by many others!

Her one-year trial period came to an end, and with the bishop's permission, Father van Exem asked Mother Teresa to write a rule of life for the new community. She wrote it in one night!

To the three customary vows taken by monks and nuns (poverty, chastity, obedience), she added a fourth: service to the poorest of the poor. The religious habit of the Missionaries of Charity was to be a white sari with three blue borders, symbolizing both the Trinity and the Virgin Mary.

A few months later, on October 7, 1950, the feast of Our Lady of the Rosary (which would also become the feast day of the order), Mother Teresa's heart was filled with immense joy: Pope Pius XII had just officially approved the new congregation of the Missionaries of Charity!

Jesus' request was at last a reality!

Gathering In the Dying

One winter's day in 1952, Mother Teresa was devastated by the sight of a dying old woman, lying in the street, with rats starting to sniff around her.

Without hesitation, she took her in her arms and carried her to the nearest hospital—where she was abruptly turned away. But Mother Teresa insisted so much that the doctor finally gave in and took care of the poor woman.

But that day put an idea in Mother Teresa's head: to find somewhere to take in the people dying in the streets. She went to the city authorities, who let her have use of an old building of the Kalighat Temple, dedicated to the Hindu goddess Kali. It had once been a shelter for Hindu pilgrims, but by then was being used only by vagabonds and drug dealers.

With the young sisters who were joining her in ever growing numbers, Mother Teresa cleaned and furnished this building, which was later to become so famous all over the world!

In this place, thanks to Mother Teresa, thousands of the dying have left this world in peace, tenderly cared for, and thus in the knowledge of Jesus' great love for them.

"I Thirst"

At the same time, the life of the sisters was organized like life in a convent, centered on prayer and service to the poor: "Prayer is the breath of life to our soul; holiness is impossible without it," Mother Teresa said. The schedule she made for her order included personal prayer, daily Mass, and Eucharistic adoration. And yet, over many long years, she herself secretly lived a Dark Night. Ever since she had moved into the slums, she no longer felt the closeness of Jesus she had before. She felt abandoned by God. She felt the loneliness Jesus experienced on the Cross. But she remained faithful throughout this trial. She continued to pray and to trust in God.

As a constant reminder to the sisters that it was Jesus himself whom they served in the poor, Mother Teresa had the words "I thirst" written on the wall next to the large crucifix in the convent chapel.

All the houses of the order have these words Jesus spoke on the Cross in their chapels.

Some Hindus from the neighboring temple saw Mother Teresa and her sisters as rivals for the people's loyalty and affection. They stirred up a riot, and police were needed to protect the sisters. But a little later, one of the Hindu leaders of the trouble contracted leprosy. When everyone else abandoned him, Mother Teresa took him in. After that, things changed. Good relations were established with the Hindus, who saw that the sisters welcomed all the poor, regardless of their religion.

I THIRST

19

All Life Is Sacred

One day in 1955, Mother Teresa discovered with horror a tiny little child abandoned in the street. It had just been attacked by a dog! She gathered up the child, lovingly nursed it, and a few days later founded an orphanage. People began bringing Mother Teresa little children, infants, wrapped in old rags or even just paper. The sisters would then baptize the children and care for them until they could be adopted by couples who were overjoyed to have at last a little girl or boy!

To Mother Teresa, all life was sacred. A little baby, even before its birth, as well as its mother, had to be protected, especially when the mother was in difficult circumstances: "Life is God's life in us, even in an unborn child."

The smaller and more destitute the poor, the more Mother Teresa wished to protect them. Did Jesus not tell us: "As you did it to one of the least of these my brethren, you did it to me"?

The Donations Flow In

Ten years had gone by since Mother Teresa had left the Sisters of Loreto to care for the poor. The new congregation continued to grow: young women in ever greater numbers joined her, and Mother Teresa now envisioned opening houses outside the diocese of Calcutta.

And so, in 1960, several missions were founded in other regions of India: New Delhi, Asansol, and Mumbai. But that took money. Mother Teresa never had a penny on her, always trusting God to provide, and teaching the sisters to do the same. And money came whenever they needed it. One day, for example, she was invited to speak on the BBC, the British radio. She spoke about what she was doing in India, and took the opportunity to ask for help. And donations flowed in on the spot! Mother Teresa reminded her listeners that one does not need to go to India to help the poor. People in need of love are all around us, she said, even in our own families.

In 1965, when Mother Teresa wanted to found a center to take in lepers, those rejected by all, Pope Paul VI, who was making a visit to India, met her and gave her his beautiful car! Without delay, Mother Teresa put it up for auction. With the proceeds, she was able to begin construction of the lepers' center right away. The same pope asked Mother Teresa to establish a presence in South America, and in Rome as well, for in Western countries there are many poor people abandoned and rejected by all. Mother Teresa opened houses on every continent: in Venezuela,

Tanzania, the Philippines, Haiti, and the United States. People called her "the Mother without borders."

It was during this same period that she also founded the Missionary of Charity Brothers, as well as the contemplative sisters and brothers who, in the silence of prayer, support the work of those serving the poor. From then on, the whole world looked with admiration on this little nun, frail and tiny but overflowing with love for the poor.

The Nobel Peace Prize

I n Oslo, Norway, on December 10, 1979, Mother Teresa was awarded the prestigious Nobel Peace Prize, which she accepted, she said, "for the glory of God and in the name of the poor." Hardly had she arrived, when she learned that a great banquet was to be held in her honor. Her reaction was immediate: how could she take part in this fine dinner, she who thought only of people dying of hunger in Calcutta? She asked that the banquet be canceled and the money used instead to feed four hundred people for a whole year. And that is what happened.

Then in the glare of the world's spotlights, the little sister stepped humbly forward and began her stirring speech by reciting Saint Francis' prayer for peace:

Lord, make [me] a channel of Thy peace that,
where there is hatred, I may bring love;
that where there is wrong, I may bring the spirit of forgiveness;
that, where there is discord, I may bring harmony;
that, where there is error, I may bring truth;
that, where there is doubt, I may bring faith;
that, where there is despair, I may bring hope;
that, where there are shadows, I may bring light;
that, where there is sadness, I may bring joy.

Lord, grant that I may seek rather to comfort than to be comforted,
to understand than to be understood;
to love than to be loved;
for it is by forgetting self that one finds;
it is [by] forgiving that one is forgiven;
it is by dying that one awakens to eternal life.

She went on to say that, in the evening of our lives, all of us will be judged on love: material aid, she insisted, counts much less than the caring, all-embracing love for the people around us.

She recalled "that man whom we picked up from the drain, half eaten with worms, and we brought him to the home.'I have lived like an animal in the street,' he said, 'but I am going to die like and angel, loved and cared for.' And it was so wonderful to see the greatness of that man who could speak like that, who could die like that. ... like an angel" Like the thousands of others cared for in her hospice, he "died a beautiful death. They have just gone home to God," she said.

Mother Teresa concluded her Oslo speech by stressing the duty to protect little babies threatened by death even before their birth, and to help expectant mothers. She encouraged those who are not ready to be mothers to give their infants up for adoption, for so many couples cannot have children of their own and long to become parents.

Mother Teresa was strongly supported by Pope John Paul II, who shared her deep concern for the unborn. He asked her to become the Church's spokesperson on the subject.

Contagious Generosity

Mother Teresa's remarkable example inspired great outbursts of generosity. The people of Calcutta had long been in the habit of leaving out a bowl of rice from time to time for beggars, a bit of rice that was of course immediately picked up. But after Mother Teresa had lived among them for a while, at the foot of the trees where people used to leave a few alms for the poor, great quantities of food—fruit and rice in abundance—were piled high!

Mother Teresa continued to found houses around the world. In 1980 and the years that followed, the Missionaries of Charity opened about fifteen houses each year, and some of these were in countries where missionaries had until then been forbidden: Ethiopia, Russia, Albania, China, and even Yemen, which had been deprived of any Christian presence for more than eight hundred years! Mother Teresa's sisters did so much good for the poor, without getting involved in religion or politics, so how could they not be welcomed?

And who could suggest that, in this, she was not witnessing to the infinite love of Jesus for all?

29

Mother Teresa did not really want donors—even very generous ones—what she wanted was "cooperators," people who would commit themselves to practice loving and attentive charity to those around them. For it's not necesssary to go to the other side of the world: the unfortunate are so often those right among us!

"Love is born and lives in the home," she said. "The absence of this love in families creates suffering and misfortune in the world today." Real love must be restored through things that may seem insignificant but that, in reality, change everything—cheerfulness, a smile, a visit, a little letter, and always, above all, kindness, even when it's difficult: "Holiness grows so fast where there is kindness."

At the end of her life, Mother Teresa continued traveling to visit the order's houses and, despite her increasingly failing health, founding new ones. Warnings from doctors ought to have slowed down her activities, but how do you extinguish Love?

Despite her numerous travels, it was in Calcutta, where it had all begun, that she departed "to go home, to God's home," as she said. She passed away on September 5, 1997, at the age of eighty-seven. Her tomb in Calcutta, in the chapel of the Missionaries of Charity, very quickly became a place of pilgrimage, even for non-Christians, for rich and poor—all so touched by her faith and charity.

Mother Teresa was beatified in Saint Peter's Basilica in Rome by Pope John Paul II on October 19, 2003, and was declared a saint on September 4, 2016, by Pope Francis.

Timeline

August 26, 1910
Mother Teresa was born as Anjezë (in English, Agnes) Gonxhe Bojaxhiu in Skopje (Macedonia).

September 28, 1928
At the age of eighteen, she left Albania to join the missionary Order of the Sisters of Loreto in Ireland. She was sent to India two months later.

1931
She took temporary vows and received the name Sister Mary Teresa.

May 24, 1937
She professed her perpetual vows.

August 17, 1948
Leaving the convent and dressing in a sari, Mother Teresa moved into the slum to show Jesus' love for the poor.

1949
She wrote the rule of life for her new community, and many women joined her.

October 7, 1950
Pope Pius XII officially approved the new congregation of the Missionaries of Charity.

1960
Seven other missions were founded in other regions of India.

1963
Mother Teresa founded the Missionaries of Charity Brothers.

1976
She began the contemplative branch of the sisters (they pray for the sisters working with the poor).

1979
She established the Contemplative Brothers.
In December, Mother Teresa was awarded the prestigious Nobel Peace Prize.

Beginning in 1980
The Missionaries of Charity opened about fifteen houses each year around the world.

1984
She established the Missionaries of Charity Fathers (priests).

1997
Mother Teresa passed away at the age of eighty-seven.
Her sisters numbered about four thousand, spread across 610 foundations throughout the world.

October 19, 2003
She was beatified in Saint Peter's Basilica in Rome by Pope John Paul II.

September 4, 2016
Mother Teresa was declared a saint by Pope Francis.

Mother Teresa is commemorated on September 5, the date of her birth in heaven.